fourteen poems

Issue 1

Hello and welcome to the very first issue of Fourteen Poems, a collection of the best new queer poets, sourced from across the planet.

Fourteen Poems has two main ambitions.

Number One: to shine a light on the most exciting LGBT+ voices and experiences right now. If you're a member of the LGBT+ community, we hope you find something familiar in these poems about your own experience.

But we'll be ecstatic if you find something new from this diverse group, something that challenges and makes you think again about the diversity of our lives.

Number Two: to make poetry accessible to all. By keeping it short and sweet, we're hoping you'll take these poems with you on your train journeys, your commutes and your day-to-day life.

We want you to dip in and out when you want a break from endless social media scrolling. Or sit down and consume it all at once, hungrily, from cover to cover. If you're feeling isolated and lonely, we hope you'll connect with a particular poem take something strengthening from them. Fourteen Poems is just a template for you to enjoy.

I dreamt up this journal imagining Sylvia Plath reading Butt Magazine, and I hope we're delivering something close to that, with poets contributing from across the planet to discuss love, sex, religion and race with a queer sensibility.

We're always taking submissions for the next issue. Check out www.fourteenpoems.com to find out how to submit and tell us about your queer poetry heroes via social media.

Enjoy,
Ben Townley-Canning

Instagram: @14poems
Twitter: @fourteenpoems

contents:

Max Wallis is an internationally renowned, award-shortlisted poet who's interested in getting poetry into places it's not normally seen. His first book of poetry *Modern Love* was nominated for the Polari Prize, and he has been described as a "poetry wunderkind" by Curious Arts Festival.

As well as being widely published in both poetry journals and magazines, Wallis has written for the Guardian, The Independent, and Elle. He is currently working on a series of crossover fantasy novels, gay literary fiction and memoir.

In 2017 he had poetry published by Vogue, did a talk at the Royal Opera House about heartbreak, collaborated with Topman twice, producing specially curated art pieces and poetry for their shows, wrote poetry for Burberry, and turned the underground at Regent's Park gay with poetry.

His second book, *Everything Everything*, is a limited edition art piece, hand bound and typeset; it looks at millennial sexuality with a blast of reality. "Read this book," - Russell T Davies.

He writes a column for Attitude Magazine.

www.max-wallis.com

Dearest Love let me tell you things

so that when you lie next to me and have a night terror legs running
like a marathon against love, you will not question what day it is
what night might have turned inside you like a tilt-shift world
so that you might hold the sun in one fist to show it me when
all I am and all I see is the cold wash of a February night - dearest love

I say this for you because you do it for me every day
so often have I been blind to those who lift me to those
who hold my paw like an injured rabid dog who wants nothing but to
bite at the whole world to feel the gnawed bone bleed - oh, love
you mean everything to me - so let me tell you things
like how when you cry it wounds me, but i can tell our friends on one hand
the times you cried that made me fall in love for you again, again, again
let me carry you like a vowel, so that you will fit in each word i place,
let me hold you in spite of myself
let me build a house of water, stabilise the very molecules of it so that each
brick, each oblong depth
of surface tension holds our love up on little pedestals so that we can be a
totem in a city
so that when the world breaks apart, when London's ravaged, there will be a
house for us
a little place with all the animals who've taken over, the ivy spilling out of our
windows, the rotting
tree trunk in our kitchen, and they will say, oh my world they loved they lived
they lived they lived

dearest love let me tell you things
we did
how we lived

Max Wallis

Dena Igusti (she/they) is a queer non-binary Indonesian Muslim poet and playwright based in Queens, New York. She is the co-founder of arts collective UNCOMMON;YOU and Short Line Review. She is a 2018 NYC Youth Poet Laureate Ambassador and 2019 Player's Theatre Resident Playwright for her co-written Off-Broadway production *Sharum*. She has performed at The Brooklyn Museum, The Apollo Theater, and more. Her forthcoming collection will be published with Game Over Books in 2020.

denaigusti.com
Twitter and IG: @dispatchdena

in case my mother tries to pull you away from me

here's the plan:
i drag my feet against the
scuffed floorboards
skin and wood splintering
into hydras of themselves

                                        where she pulls i pull
                                            twice as hard,
                                          whether that be
                                          knee buckled so
                                         forward my shins
                                        bend like the legs
                                            of a crane
                                              or arm

dislocated just to
break away
from its creator
my mama made
me and can take me
out but i can take
myself out too

                                         if my mother's grip
                                            is too strong
                                        as it always has been
                                        i'll gnaw off her wrist
                                          and let her hand
                                        squeeze my shoulder
                                        if she wants to always
                                            be with me
                                         i'll give her this

after i break loose
from the rest of my mother
i'll shove the essentials
in a suitcase:
eyeliner to draw your favorite
dots under my eyes,
ponds moisturizer,
a toothbrush,
our harness,
and a pair of hoop earrings

when my mother
unfurls her scream
like smoke
i'll take a deep breath
let her rattle in my
ribcage
hack my lungs to
secondhand tar
but still run down the stairs,
bag and a part of my mother
in tow

all you must do
is keep the engine warm
the passenger door open
and arms outstretched
so you can hold me
as i cry till nothing but
air comes out my mouth

i hope you still take
me with you
i hope you still want this me:
all fight and bite
remnants of my mother
both genetic and just taken after
nothing to give you
but what you've known of me
up to this

to love you is
to know my mother won't stay
to love you is
to know she won't let me go
but here i am
pressed against your skin
not asking my mother to leave
but telling her that

i too, can't remain

Dena Igusti

8

Rowena Knight's poetry is influenced by her identity as a queer feminist and her childhood in New Zealand. Her poems have appeared in various publications, including Butcher's Dog, Magma, The Rialto, and The Emma Press Anthology of Love. She was shortlisted for the 2018 Bridport Prize and commended in the 2019 Winchester Poetry Prize. Her first pamphlet, *All the Footprints I Left Were Red*, was published with Valley Press in 2016. She tweets @purple_feminist.

Fortune Teller Fish

hesitates at the warmth of my palm
before rolling into a coil.

The wonderful magic tell the fortune.
Curls up entirely........Passionate.

She rocks softly as though afraid
— missing her neat plastic envelope

the typed instructions setting her straight.
Moving head and tail........In love.

Childhood crushes were performance, a means
of slipping into the school. Like a Mercury Bay rucksack

everyone had to have one. Now I work hard
to give nothing away, keep the gossip

sealed under my skin. It's a full-time job
when her hair's pouring down like a spotlight and she reaches

across the table to squeeze my hand.
It takes everything not to crimp to a crimson

pretzel. I want to call in sick,
it's too hard pretending to have legs

when I'm a limp trout hypnotised
on a bed of ice. Even this plastic sliver

sprung from a cracker feels like a sister
as it twitches on my hand, helpless with static.

I've never been so parched as when she tips
her head back, her neck a long glass of water.

The fish lurches drunkenly and dives from my hand.
The heat's too much for her, poor minnow.

She doesn't know how to navigate
this sickly, tinsled air, she's thirsty

for her cool blue world. But there's no going back
after the snap, gunpowder hook

in the back of your throat,
the first breath of her cigarette.

Rowena Knight

dom schwab is a reader/writer of poetry/prose, a bearded ginger and happily partnered. dom identifies as gay/queer and his poetry often explores failed homosexual encounters & unrequited gay love. dom's poems have appeared online & in print, most recently on ExPat Press' website (*To Search & Suggest*) & Tiny TOE Press' ::the open end:: (*3 poems*). dom lives a quiet life with his boyfriend in Chicago & rarely uses Twitter (@domschwab) & Instagram (@domschwab303).

Fire

"I just want to fuck," he purrs, coaxing
an urge which before only sparingly
arose to greet my conscious, timid mind.

The small of his back, bent
in a practiced way, is locked,
posing plump & round an ass
that surely has been trained for this:
too inviting & expectant
for it to serve, at least for now,
some other end but pleasure…

Forgiveness arrives swiftly for
he vaguely comprehends what he's done,
but, afterward, in each other's arms,
he will know it worked.

Dom Schwab

Jonah Henry (he/him) is a daydreamer, poet and bookworm from Los Angeles, California. He's currently a spoken word performer for Get Lit – Words Ignite, a young adult poetry troupe, with whom he'll create his first chapbook in the summer of 2020.

[first sleepover ends in earthquake]

in the fairytale our mom always tells us before bed,
we aren't scared of earthquakes. we're young   hungover
and the buzz from our birth hasn't worn off
your mouth on my neck in the rhythm
that would make a man fall to the floor for scotch
or god's mercy but not those of us who've
only gone to church for funerals   those of us who
once rested our shoulders on a man's heart or playground fence
and couldn't be
          resurrected

sunup over our first sleepover and we leap
back into our own
bedframes   drape blankets over the glare that could've been dad's
lamp   scared of the dark but never of the
shadows   our ghosts left
your tongue scraped but built with a
bumblebee parade from our front yard   garden
we can't love ourselves if we don't have
stung fingers   and honey all over our teeth
dad warned me I shouldn't go to bed undressed
one shoulder away from a boy who plays
guitar for our school band   every creak of the floorboard enough for a
boy to cry
wolf   told me a story about the black bears who crept onto front porches in the
          forest
hometown he was born in and the men
who carry rifles under their mattress from
now on   dad warned me boys are raped too
though not if they're careful
dad warned me i've always had a sweet tooth and   it's true
even now   my dear
strewn across the torn carpet we haven't sewn together you are
every candy bar i've ever snuck into mom's grocery cart
you are   all the bedsheets i've put at the

bottom of the laundry
dad told me what's a body if not a
temple   and if god's   every two boys who've
made love before us and the world
they built with their
own four palms   (my dear we   rattled
an earthquake out of the walls as if we were   god
ourselves)
then we both must be   a priest
repeat every gasp as   chorus

sunup over our first
accident
and we   leap back into the glare that could've been dad's   bonfire
but it wasn't
remember we've locked our door with
hammers and dad's bolts so the
smoke couldn't escape   so the smoke wouldn't
set off the fire alarms
remember the toolboxes we'd used to pry off the
buttons on each other's   clothes
how urgently we loved
from a cage or padlock
of your cut tongue and black eyes   the ones I gave you
in the sandbox   how natural it was
to call two boys on top of each other   a wrestle
how many more wounds
it saved us   my dear we   gifted love out of an
earthquake   scared dad   out of los angeles
queer body   never was a stranger with
earthquakes
how urgently we   loved in a campground with bears outside the
tent   the fabric   too heavy for even us
how urgently we loved
how urgently we loved
how urge   fought us until sunup

Jonah Henry

Jonah Pontzer is a queer American painter living and working in London. You can follow him on instagram at @p0ntz3r

What we knew of love

we left to crust in tube socks
beneath beds we slept in alone
For fear of ever being loved,
Deeply, for who we are yet
To become and still to forget.

Jonah Pontzer

Kyron Rizzo is a queer student-athlete of colour at Wesleyan University, from Brooklyn, New York. Within the LGBT+ community Kyron Rizzo identifies as gay, nonbinary, ace, and also dem (it's a mouthful...so they mostly stick with queer). In addition to poetry, Rizzo loves to pop jokes, dance, and watch anime. You can follow Rizzo on almost all social media platforms at @kyron.rizzo, they're particularly active on Instagram, Tiktok, and YouTube.

For Colored Boiz

For colored boiz
For queer colored boiz
For innocent...

Funkdafied
Independent
Intellectual
loving
Colored boiz

> who rock to Betty Davis
> And Durand Bernarr

> Down in the paint
> Getting crucified like a saint

Don't let another false prophet
tell ya u caint

Light sage
And Expel demon from cage

Embers press against skin
Like nagging kin

> Slow to burn
> Peeling back layers
> Having left their mark

> Slow to learn
> Whisper of prayers
> Left to fall silent in the dark

But Black skin that shines
Ain't hard to find
Shea and coconut been clearing ash from bruised rinds
....

> They say I'm different 'cause I'm sweet like Black berry and Red kool aid
> They say I'm different 'cause I eat ass and suck dick

But that won't have braids unravelling here sis
I can't help it if I was born different

But my daddy don't care
Because he loves me for real
And he'd do anything for his little queer colored boi

Say I'm different 'cause I'm sweet like black berry and Red kool aid
Say I'm different 'cause I eat ass and suck dick
....
But don't play coy
run on Colored Boi

That's right, different

That's right, strange

when I/u walk, I/u strut
When I/u talk, I/u can make a nigga blush
Chassé, serve face, Don't play,
Coons still outche lookin suus

Mouths Wide shut
Zip and hush

Running laps around bros
Leaving unchecked stares
In the dust

Busting out the closet on the seventh day
Having them fall to their knees.. Struck

Put your records on Colored boiz
Get floetic if u have to
Cause isn't that what charlie always want u to do

But remember
You're a wash n set away
From pressed to decompressed
From stressed to damn near fearless

Moisturize
Leave in
And Repeat

...
Charlies
Outchea lookin for a eunuch
Take a seat
.....

Ease your mind colored boi
Easy your mind

....
Stop cradling limp dick
docked on mom and pops shriveling tit
....
Hear queer colored boi talk
Air go flat and have the nerve to scoff
Niggas forget, like nut, they small and quick to finish off

...
But isn't it like a queer colored boi to flick em off with the shrug

....
Eyes tightly coiled
Whilst Charlie screaming icon-n-e-c-k
Heck
gotta recoil
laugh from chest
Scrunched mouth from neck

Lest I get rickety wrecked
Tagged
And checked

Again...

Queer Colored Boiz
Don't Forget to do ya best and speak from the chest
...

And if you're from the ghetto
Let us harmonize whilst we speak in falsetto

Kyron Rizzo

Lotte Thomson-Vock is a queer writer from Sydney, Australia. She has previously written for the literary zine Flash Fiction. Lotte also writes about art for non-fiction publications Art Pharmacy and Megaphone Oz.

Nylon

Breath smells cleaner when I take it from your mouth

Morning dew kissing my toes where the macadamia nuts fell

Too hard to eat raw

A state-wide fire ban – can't throw them on hot coals

Wildfire roars a suburb away

But I am lying in your underarm

Dimpled smile makes a sucking noise like the collapse of the universe

A cacophony of birds and grumbling gravel beyond the cheap plastic crinkle of my sleeping bag

Over our heads

Concave dreaming of crescent moons

A nail clipping snapped into the blanket of darkness

Against the tapestry of stars

Nylon dreams and anxious thoughts about mozzies

Your ankles bitten raw

Miniature pink peaches weeping into your toes with

sediment clogging up at the knuckles of your footprints

Nylon dreams about kissing you

Kissing your weeping mosquito bites, your dirty toes

A midnight barefoot dance twisting into filth

Licking my poisoned lips

I squeeze the mosquitos trapped in my gut and lodge them in my throat accidentally

I kiss your morning breath

Over you, my saliva falls into your mouth and you swallow

Hands feel like strange play things

Flaccid wrists stiffen like grilled cuttlefish

Squeaky chewy cartilage diced like hugs (O) and broken kisses(/ \ / \ | \ / |)

fresh sloppy cuttlefish wetness filed in between you and I turn the creased dog eared
pages of your lips

Licking my forefinger and thumb

The anxiety of eyes under nylon shadows

My fingers where they shouldn't be

nervous inside of you

I fight the feeling we're being watched

Familiar low voices subvert your moan and

I grab your mouth with my dirty fingers

A tent stirs and I hide my dripping mollusc fingers back beside your immovable
body

I hear you hold breath

Hiding the buzzing of mosquitos now under my hands

Gnawing pink peaches in my undies

Lotte Thomson-Vock

Alyssa Romero Kibiloski is a queer poet, writer, musician, and artist living in Los Angeles. Currently, she is finishing her first poetry anthology, *Cutting Hair*, which is organised by the length of her hair over the last decade. You can find Alyssa on walkabouts in Echo Park, fingering her pockets for a mantra acorn or stone, running up trail ridges, indulging her vegan sweet tooth, dancing as a form of connecting back to self, writing melodic intimate melodies, graphic designing, and painting on found objects. Follow her and her work on instagram @a.ro.k

Aries Son

I was going to be a son

came into the room a moon
crescent eyed and full
head of hair
still curling and wild
with teeth of pixels
gunshot ascents
green destruction

my thorns are louder

desiring like walking
feeling like breathing
in one exhale

last week three coyotes crossed my path
and turned their heads
never breaking stride
that is how I want to live

alive, the negative space between you
and the glass door
a flower where this is no flower

Alyssa Romero Kibiloski

Tamara Natt (she/her) is a queer poet, essayist and playwright living with her wife on the semi-rural Australian coastline. Her work, spanning her beat poetry play *ALPHA* (Edinburgh Fringe Festival) to *A Letter to Everyone I Have Ever Met*, an online project that interrogates the significance of first impressions, is deeply personal, highly political and brutally romantic.

Instagram: @tamara.natt

Dear Mandy Moore

Dear Mandy Moore –
And all of the other girls
I loved
At high school,

During late night landline
Phone calls
When I stung my throat
Giving you advice
About your thick-necked boyfriends
Over the racket
Of my softly-spoken heart
Breaking politely

And noticing your hips
In your swimmers –
Oh shit.

And saying good morning
To your hopeless fathers.

And planning
How I would rescue you –

I'm sorry
I never found the courage
To love you
Out loud,

And left you
To the mercy
Of patio renovations
And coffee catch-ups
With the girls

But
Do you still think of me
Late a night
When your landline rings?

Yours,
Tamara Natt
2020

Tamara Nett

Peter Scalpello (he/him) is a gay poet and sexual health therapist from Glasgow, currently living and working in East London. His work is also featured and forthcoming in Pilot Press, harana poetry, Sonic Boom, POLARI, New River Press, Visual Verse and Fruit Journal, and by the Show Me Yours Prize and HIV Humanities, University of Manchester. Tweets @p_scalpello.

little soy sauce fish bottle
fixed with GBL,
pleasure buds an unbound nozzle
spouts vitreous, a miniscule relief

invisible, really   squeeze down
your eager thumbs &
was it even there?

what's 2ml to
man, tattoos that score the width
of a heaving torso

one lucid bream to ravage inhibition
subdue dysfunction, arrest
your forever fervent aorta,

arrest forever your—

little zesty puddle of
impetus, distilled

we drop we do it with
irony

Peter Scalpello

Slam The Poet is a queer writer who is fascinated with the sensuality of words - their sights, sounds & textures. They see poetry as a hugely flexible art form and have followed their curiousity through music, fine art, and theatre with a thirst for experimentation deeply rooted in a joy for collaboration. This has included work with STEEZ, Brainchild Festival, Promundo Global, Half Moon Theatre and Apples & Snakes. You can find more of them at slamthepoet.com or @slamthepoe on facebook and instagram.

Panic Attack on London Bridge (after Ocean Vuong)

And isn't it such a painless terror?
The people so busy
you pass right through them,
thinking you have found air. As if
no mind could hold you still
no ghost could fix you.
Eyes lost in the rupture,
the falling moment
of forever.

> *There are days*
> *when the world*
> *is covered in knives*
> *and I don't eat*
> *for fear of my kitchen.*

Please Tom, don't be scared.
Don't pretend to believe it lasts.
You are already relinquishing it
for the next. Slowing into a moment
when your stillness is all you have
to hold yourself together
as you imagine the collision
of a mismatched journey,
the sweat, a mist
on your palms.

Slam The Poet

Carissa Cancel (they/them/their) is currently based out of a small Nassau County town in New York. This gender-queer, pansexual Latinx covers the good, the bad, and the extremely personal happenings of life quickly approaching 30. When they're not spilling their heart out in poetry, you can find them lost in a good book, cooking some good food up, or finding peace in the outdoors. Carissa's work can be found on Instagram at @cm.cancel.

Abyss

There are galaxies worth of
oceans inside of my chest.
I feel their tides change with every breath.

Inhale, shallow or deep.
The swell of their waters are skyscraper high.
Exhale, slowly and all at once
into beautiful, devastating monsoons.

Fearful my dams can no longer
keep them from rushing out of me
and I have forgotten how to swim.

Carissa Cancel

Jahan Khajavi (b. 1986, Fresno) is a poet & MFA candidate in Creative Writing at the University of Notre Dame who writes "wildly amusing & explicit queer poetry" (Hamish Bowles, Vogue) informed by classical Persian traditions. When not in South Bend, Jahan lives & works in Rome with recent performances there at the Swiss Institute, Gavin Brown's Enterprise, & Silvia Fendi's backyard. Jahan is also the host of Suddenly Every Wednesday—a weekly radio program featuring live on-air literary readings from 10pm to Midnight EST on WSND 88.9FM—& organizes the Bricks Reading Series at the Crossroads Gallery.

The Ass Within the Ass

i.

Our beloved is as golden-eyed & young as that famed Pharaoh,

spitting image of the sun, while our beloved's lover is

as old as Siam.

                Our beloved is that celebrated arrow

Arash shot around the World & our beloved's lover is

the dew damp spot it struck; the grassy floor upon which our beloved,

faun-like, slopes into a stony sleep.

                        A page ripped right from Ovid!

How could such a new moon beauty such as them, a spritely sparrow,

fall for this stuffed eagle head that our beloved's lover is?

ii.

Dearest reader, if you so desire to divine

the legal name of our beloved, powpow pound it out

of our beloved's lover!

                Reed into our skin a sign,

the sole who popo-potentially has ever found it out;

or finger us a flute & force our flesh to sing the unsung

vowels: from A to eye-hole; even better you, with tongue

papa pad prep pressed against the braille—pree pree printed fine—

of our beloved's lover's hemorrhoids inflamed, may sound it out.

iii.

We can swallow all of this world's bitterness

like Persian tea with them upon our tongue.

                        They're sweet, but

not too much—a sugar in the mind, no less;

the kind that sometimes sours in the mouth.

                        They're sweet, but

in the way that wine is haram—we confess

that though each day of ours is Ramadan, we fast

while sucking on the dream that night will come, at last;

that hour when we can devour their sweet butt.

iv.

If our beloved's lover took another shape,

it'd be as a lone hair on our beloved's ass;

or else a gnat—not gnawing, but napping on their nape—

or pair of underwear on our beloved's ass

to hold them—even for a brief—to bear them up,

unbare their fruit, to loom—to be the saqi's cup!

But we—inside this body that we can't escape—

can only fix our stare on our beloved's ass.

v.

No more poems!

                Our beloved's lover's moving hand

can't write, of course, while buried deep in our beloved's rectum.

See those three coarse hairs above their booty hole?

                                            They stand

& sing of treasure buried deep in our beloved's rectum!

If we thought it would deliver us, without delay,

we'd swiftly carve out our own liver on the spot—the way

Mishima reached his throne the moment that he threw his hand—

so that we may be buried deep in our beloved's rectum.

Jahan Khajavi